A PORTFOLIO OF DEFIANCE:

*

Of dream poems, echo poems, poem chants, voice poetry, poetry painting poems, sketch poems, essays poems, visual poetry, music poetry, photographic poetry, word poetry, number poetry, verses poetry, story poetry...

Tendai Rinos Mwanaka

Typeset by Tendai Rinos Mwanaka
Cover: **The Windman Kittiwakes© Tendai Rinos Mwanaka**

Mwanaka Media and Publishing Pvt Ltd,
Chitungwiza Zimbabwe

*

Creativity, Wisdom and Beauty

Publisher: Tendai R Mwanaka

Mwanaka Media and Publishing Pvt Ltd *(Mmap)*

24 Svosve Road, Zengeza 1

Chitungwiza Zimbabwe

mwanaka@yahoo.com

www.africanbookscollective.com/publishers/mwanaka-media-and-publishing

https://facebook.com/MwanakaMediaAndPublishing/

Distributed in and outside N. America by African Books Collective

orders@africanbookscollective.com

www.africanbookscollective.com

ISBN: 978-1-77906-481-3

EAN: 9781779064813

DISCLAIMER

All views expressed in this publication are those of the author and do not necessarily reflect the views of *Mmap*.

iii

Table of Contents

Introduction

Every few years I go through an artistic journey or phase in my life, and this collection deepens the phase I went through between 2009-2016 and in the process I produced 4 collections: *Logbook Written by a Drifter* (2009-2010), *Revolution: Struggle Poems* (2011-2012), this one *A Portfolio of Defiance* (2013-2014) and *When Escape Becomes the Only Lover* (2014-2016). Looking at the phase after some few years these collections have a number of strong issues they share.

The first is experimentation and innovativeness in the writing. In each of these collections I tried to be a scientist, by experimenting with forms, styles, with subject matter too. Poets should be scientists, should continuously try to find new ways of writing, to problematicise what we have always taken for granted.

The second aspect related to experimentation, is to try to understand and critically dissect how art criticism and actual art can be mixed in poem form. A number of poems in this anthology straddles that meeting point, for instance these 4 poems, *Whet girl, black boy; Words; Sands of Time: This is my House; The Hyena in Me, Voices*. Whilst writing these poems I also irreverently treated issues to do with the meaning of words, what words are, I create new words, what numbers are, the state of voice, language, thoughts, dreams, perspectives, life, race, death, spirituality, love etc...

Still related to experimentation, the storytelling tradition is strong in these 4 anthologies too, especially in this one and *Revolution: Struggle Poems*. What I am saying is poets are also storytellers, who tell a story in condensed form with depth of thought and feeling. A number of poems in this anthology uses the storyteller's eye, for instance, *The Living Room; Dreams, Paintings, Light; Old Man, Dreams, Writing; Two Children…*

The other important aspect is defiance. Each anthology is defiant. I refuse to settle on anything, to accept anything, I am a literary rebel with language, with writing, that's why I succinctly entitled this collection *A Portfolio of Defiance*, and the part title says it all, "*Of dream poems, echo poems, poem chants, voice poetry, poetry painting poems, sketch poems, essays poems, visual poetry, music poetry, photographic poetry, word poetry, number poetry, verses poetry, story poetry…*".

I create poetry with anything!

There is no taboo subject in this collections. I dealt with Satanism in *The Alter of the Dark*, I dealt with Child abuse in *Stations of the Cross* and mixed this issue with Jesus's suffering, I dealt with numbers and words, their Hermeneutic alchemy in *1-9*, I dealt with sex, love and relationships in *Place of Love*, I dealt with the world of phantasy and the strange in *Two Children*, I dealt with dreams in several pieces too.

In all these collections, especially in this one we can see that the poet is trying to understand his voice. The longest piece and I think the most experimental in this collection is entitled *Voices*. It investigates voices before voice, and voices after voice and the world in between. What was it like when there was no voice on earth? What will it be like when all voices are dead on earth? It asks what a human being would really be without voice. Is that the world of nothingness? And as the poet closes the collection with these words,

"Can you tell yourself by the trails I have left across these definitions?
Addressing yourself
As a no one

As a no person
As nothing"
    We want to say nothingness is a voice too!

White Girl, black boy

The human skin is now the only existing surface
That has conquered millennials of self-recognition, of revelation,
    Elevation…
The dermis has become a convener of beingness, as a surface
It both limits, *and* interrupts the contours of the landscape and
flesh

    And after a few years (after what), I am still debating whether
    the skin is the only existing surface that has survived a history
    of *cut and paste manifest destiny*. The human mind, my mind tells
    me, instead of the dermis, or in abidance of the skin, has
    become an interlocutor of sensing, of presencing, as a surface.
    Surface, senses, surfacing, the S of surfaces, curvy like trailway
    lines- intersecting, the mind; both jails and skyrockets the
    contours of the landscape and flesh.

I imagine, imagining my imaginations
    Like dreaming my dreams
What if white is not?
Really white!
A smudgy "pinkish" colour?
    The black *racist* chimes: *A decoration on basically an empty landscape,*

And the black boy thinks: If i was really black, i might not really be
seen.
Because I could hide things in my own blackness and if she were
really white,
When she is being white, white as genetically white (family-tree
white)
She wouldn't see me, for she would only be the wind, air

Light stripes of air, pinned around my corporeal clothes
Like cold tasting light, itself in the mouth of itself.

The white girl thinks and invests this with import: It is a black skin
muddled, annihilated of its truth.
    She thinks of the skin (nakedness) as the best possible example
    of surface,
No more his own skin; *crythematous*-patches (erythematous-batches
of), necrotic tissues-indurated, the body laminated against itself
As its skins boils in its blackness
The black thing always needing, needlingwanting, to get in the way,
Even now

Like the deadly white of the sky
She inherited the whiteness
The sugar coating whiteness
It is whiteness
As witness

The white *racist* thinks and sheriffs it, you can't deny her that: This
is what has been passed down to me
A white horned hunger to live, live and live and live…
As long as bacteria
In this whiteness
Is it whiteness as white-colouredwhite
Prosecuting…

The two, the white girl and the black boy, are talking of the cloudy
of ice-cold that is always hovering on either side of this harness, the
weave is the skin, which attempts to harness a centrality of spirit,
and the rituals each of the two enacts to cipher it out in their
relationship.
But, I will do an Alice Walker here

And I imagine, with Walker, the psychic liberation of black if it
understands
Black is not really black
I imagine, still with Walker, the exhilarating feeling of white if it
could walk (doing a Walker with me) away from the caged feeling
Of its body, in its own skins!
   I was just talking of colours, the white and black colours!

1-9

The number 1 still bores me like James Mukonoweshuro
James Mukonoweshuro was a student in my primary school grades
He always got the top spot, in the class, in the grade
Number 1
Always wanting to be the first, negating out of existence Zero, or
even negating negatives…
Negating negatives was not a positive. Thus 1 minus 2…was…*it
can't*
They were no negatives or Zero for me at primary school; to beat
James Mukonoweshuro with.
I was always number 2 or worse
2 attracted me, even now. Its angles and curves
I hated 3, because
It wasn't closer to number 1, like 2 was
It was good to know that even though he was always number 1, he
could feel me at number 2
Number 3 and he would just ignore me
The U in four (4), is yes, gives me voluptuous pleasure. Which u?
You!
Are you asking me?
I love 5, even though if you were to twist one side of it, it would
look like 3, the 3 I hated
Twisted untwisted, and twisted…is it crazy? Is 5 a normal twin of
an abnormal 3?
But 5 represent freedom (who is saying that!), adaptability (due to
the twisting and untwisting twists), unpredictable travel (in the
Himalaya mountains), and abuses of senses (when it is 3); it is 5.
Who is twisting it? It depends with whose hand(s)
Six (6)…and did he say sex…has always been interesting

It looks like an abnormal...I mean, upside down thing swimming off, to fertilize...populate her with abnormality. Pregnancy.... It's like my father was a virgin when he met my mother. So mine was a virgin birth, even though I am the second born...was the second born

I can't be the second born now

I am not in a state of perpetual birth

I can't say the second alive, to live

I stop it!

7 is boring, just like some joined kindling, or an axe, chopping off things...like on a news clip when the demented character gets hold of an axe and starts chomping off limps...of people, at a vacation outing, in the deep forests of Mississippi, as they try to flee from his axe, and call the police

It's his axe, oozing out Mississippi blood. Blue

And we watch it on the news; it is like in one of those movies. We are supposed to feel sorry for these people, but we had been told people on the television do not die

Did they catch the guy?

Nope, it is cold case

Seven is a lot of humanity, to die from an axe

It's his axe

And we were supposed to feel empathy

Seven is just too cold, seven hells, seventh hell?

It is seven with a small bar on its middle, that's a bit interesting

If you twist this one, it becomes 4

You are asking me how, really!

Sorry, I can't answer you for the sanatorium in my head (heart) has

(or   even   soul)

77777777777777777777777777777777777777777777777777777777777777

77777 beds

I mean 7 beds. The first one is for James Mukonoweshuro, mine is the second one, the third one is for you, and that's why you are reading this. The forth one has a patient in it and he is the only one physically there, a patient who is not a patient, the fifth one has a shadow in it, twisting and twisting, retilting the twists like 5. The sixth one is for your woman, girl or whatever you call her, the seventh one is an object, I mean Chinese food: dogs or snakes meat 8 is curvy. It is the most interesting number, with its sexy curves, booming out. It encloses things in its two curves

It's not inside its two circles where I would want to be, but outside of it...licking its curves...

Licking and licking ice cream

9 is a 6 raised to a standing position. Might not be as productive as sex because the tail swims off rightly, the right way....

The correct way

That is

The right way

Words!

No...

Numbers?

Maybe

WORDS

The name of a word should have permission to deal itself
Black notes dancing on white paper: words
Epileptic, Tourettic, Operatic, evened unEvened out, Issonance
Don't turn to the dictionary. It won't find me wrong, because I won't allow it. I have used them that way, Humpty dumpy, dumping... They burn that way, like a fire. She checks the dictionary page marked "Fire" to see how it burns. It is dump like water; it doesn't burn the page for her.
Some words can only be pronounced by their own selves.
Less is more, what "more"? Can I do more with less, that is more, that is less, more...? Let me tank it. Let me...
The name of words should have permission to arise from their bed with bits of their beds caught on their eyelashes. Derrida calls it the pharmakon. Hermeneutic alchemy of words...where words means themselves and their antonym; life and death, poison and medicine, fuck, cleave, fire, water, fuck this! Sorry, I gag it.
The misuse of words is the best mattress for the words, curving out an aura from their truths.
Locus (maybe Lego set) of absurd misapplication: we tie names to words, and words tie names to us, like: Dick, Charlie, and Jane... am I, a word? My name is Tendai. Does this incur a chronic alter of vowels? It is a word. It means: we thank, I thank, thanks, you thank. Thanks, thanking who; God, my parents, me, you? Tendai, how much...? Tendai Mwanaka, and how much is that?
Mwanaka means you are beautiful, you are so beautiful...
Am I?
I who am nothing more (or less) than myself?
Not my surname...
Water always speaks in its own voice, do I?
Words are bodies broken by saying them, thinking of them, writing them...

7

Do I break myself by my just being there, I mean here, speaking my name, when someone speaks it, when I think of it? Thinking that I am TendaiRinos (Rinos, not that beautiful animal with its horns, otherwise my big fat nose might be mistaken for a horn), I have a second name, that I don't like. Here (in my second name: Rinos), I am not my name but the paths that rains trails, the measure of their tumble. Haha, and *what's what* with the primitive theories of rain!
Are you now breaking me by reading this, me?
This question is lost in the questioning me
The answer is just safe words
Words strangled of their real nonsenses....
Some words beg for forgiveness for their definitions
. . . .
 I forgive?
. . . .
What?
. . . .
Words?
. . . .
Did I?

THE GUILTY TRIP

It's a careen, careening into the trail, every time we have arguments.
It's always, I didn't show her that I love her well, better, good
(which is not well), and best…I don't know which one here. It's
getting such that I feel I am upended between the hard place and a
rock. That little space changing me, the way neighborhoods
changes us, for the worse. I want to love her the way she wants me
to do it- but I want to love her the way I know how. Days when
she rapes me for not loving her, it's like I have squashed a bug by
accident. It was on its trail, rail trails on my body, and I thought it
was a dangerous and poisonous thing or a pest, like lice. I must
now repent. She persecutes me, I feel I must repent to her love, to
her sensitivity, to her woman, and I am left with so much guilty,
careening on a guilty trip, trail. Is my love a form of misuse? Not a
site for her. I am forced to keep asking for my scales back, my
animal form. I know it is always good to think through before
exploding, to cut out your darlings, but someday I will tell her off. I
would have to risk out swimming inside her heaven
I will do the *Erin Moures*, telling off her vampire cling, the need to
cling and cling in her.

Listen, Parrot, I know you are hungry (a hungry sucker for love); *and that
you don't like yourself. I know you sometimes fly.* Pup purruuu…, branch
here I sit!
I am not a parrot. I would rather you had said I am a pigeon or the
proverbial sheep in the bible, she would refuse this naming. She is a
bloody fighter.
Get a life!
What?
Change! Shift, shape up, be say, a dove (not the pigeon she wanted me to
name her) *or sparrow, a weedy plant, a furious imprecation,*
doppelganger, *a ghost,* ghamghost… what a host!

9

Really!
Her whinnying is getting on my nerves
Could I have a glass of *Valter?*

It doesn't really bother me if she changes into a ghost and climb on top of me, on my body, to receive seeding. Then I will gloss, guilty free, my cornucopian perishables here, have a roasted cob!

THE LIVING ROOM

The living room that is not
The room to loom, to leave
Reserved for the living
When to live is not a sacrifice

A sacrificial pedestal for the unliving:
Abstract paintings, unused chessboard, expensive picture frames, a lot without photos in them, one with a very old photo, one with her photo, one with an unknown girl, framed inside it…it's a picture frame. The unknown girl is praying, in a prayer, like as if before prayer. Lilith? Garden Eden isn't that. Plastic plants, liquor cabinets; with unopened bottles, maturing beer… And wine. A calendar from long ago, counting life backwards, or is it time, backwards? What time is it? 1 am, it's I: AM in the morning. Nearby a pot of sand, in it, a frozen wax candle, as if a bird was trying to pick out its own heart, with its own death beak: death, dead, die. Did she?He thinks, in the dead form, *she is my mom. My mom who is still alive.*
Death, dead, die….

Death's waters
In her religion they cooked food using water sipped after cleaning her body. They couldn't stay (the mourning woman of the street) for the food, to eat her. And, her family was supplying endless foods but there was no one left to eat her. It was witch's food. It had been cooked using the witch's waters. The place became an unwanted or unappreciated restaurant in a ghost city.

The living room is still
Its contents do not move
Make sounds, they do not!

A door, to door it

There is only one door: a back door into it or out of it; into the living room, out of the living room. Doors! To door in. There is no front door. To front in. Had there ever been a front door? Front. He sees where it should have been. Where it should have been, there is a glass door. He walks to it. It is the light from the mirror, which collects him in, into the landscape of this room. He presses his face against the glass of it, all that unrealised potential. He tries to open the glass door, but it is locked. He thought of breaking it, with his body, for broken glass predicts change, necessarily not beneficial, but he thought better of it. So, he doesn't break it. He will keep the glass mirror, for glass generally indicates a strong psychic or intuitive ability.He tries to open the glass door, but it is locked.

He goes back to get the keys.
The act of going back goes with him
It never returns back with him.
He goes back to unlock it, but it is already unlocked.
He is unlocked, he must be doors or
There must be another lock on the outside, he thinks.

The unused chessboard

He retires back into the room. He sits on the wasted grey sofa. It has stripes of greys and smaller stripes of greens that interlocks. Flowery grey.He sleeps on a couch right across the sofa he is sitting on, smaller for his long frame, so nights he sleeps on bended knees. His blankets and clothing rests on this couch, like left over dreams.He takes the chessboard, opens it. Note: the lack of him in *open it*. He populates it with ponies on the back lines, and the others (horses, bishops, castles, a queen, a king, these; always competing in

the hashed silence like cotton, by sheer will they always put themselves at the back row).
Today he puts them on the front. He wills it!

We pray to space by doing life
On the opposing side, he leaves that space open. Space is Open. Open space is a double negative, it's a positive possibility. Space denotes the world before mathematical exactitude, and the world of mathematical doubt. We play with (pray to) space by doing life. He is playing chess against himself. He jumps the pony, taught (thought) better of it, and he returns it back. He remembers; it's the horse that should jump around. Horses...
So he lets one of his horses jump...it's a long, long leap. To leap is an act of freedom. It lands well beyond her characters..., playing her things out of the game.

He waits. What colour is waiting??
When the silence starts dominating, he looks at the mirror door, the glass doors where a door should have been, was, is...

Do tears make moaning sounds?
The face on the window, dissolving, reconstituting, he doesn't like the look of the thing that looks back at him. The look of the door that looks back at him overwhelms his ability to tell her to play her move. Cold, eternal, eyes of black marble: tears trying, beginning to appear. Do tears make moaning sounds? Whoaaa, whoaaa, whoaaa... howling out a glossolalia over her death?

This living room was empty (that was empty) with a swarm of relatives, a month ago. His father, with tears in his heart, said, *The light thing has taken her.* He meant, he now thinks but doesn't know for sure, what he meant was, *nothing is more orderly than nothing.* Maybe he meant, *The dark thing has taken her.*

13

Is nothing more orderly than nothing?
We are always tied down to eye-blink half-lives. Blink blink, unsure of who or how to hold hard.

There is nothing to hold, there is no outside world, only a mirror…and the outside that is not a world. He is inside excavated-out time; phantom wind excites the outside, which is not there, perhaps; it's a slow shadow, passing. And an unseen silhouette on his mind obstructs him.

He reverts his eyes, back onto the chessboard.
She has played her hand…no, no, no…it's a move…he tells himself. Lazy eight!

This is not crazy eight!
He sits back on the vehicle of his imaginations, seeing her skip a couple of gears with her castle, accelerate with the bishop, lose grip with the pony, crash with another pony, as it lands square feet beside his queen: checkmate! The little men of the war have done their work, sacrificed for the good of the big man. She says *Checkmate*, again, she is smiling, smirking at him, her smile stinking him like a newborn's first wound, or the shock of birth. No wound prepares human beings for the loneliness in the world they empty into at birth than that first wound of birth: Birth itself! Herself. He stares at her smile again, it's a life. She is life.
It is life.
It belongs to the outside, rubbing out the blooded outside air…
She sets out to stop the air outside from hemorrhaging berries, or blood…
With her smile, of course!

Not with words

When she was here with him she would talk and talk, and it's now amazing that with so many words in her being, she hasn't set one free. Why not make use of her key (words) to utter nothing: to soften this myth machine in him, anger, the bull brute cry, bonfire as this azure, or maybe a spatula; a wedge to be woven in...
Now she is saying to ask questions and she will participate, and he says to her:
I can't get through the glass!

He cannot leave this room, live in this house...loom, room out of this room. He has taken time further inland; to sew lives' boats, thoughts' ships, and feelings' vessels. Everything floats: rugs, tables, chairs- and so do his dreams, dry fields of corn, dry riverbeds in the draught year of 1992. Everything: browner, greying, decaying...
1992, that's when he met her,

2002- Everything: browner, greying...
He no longer leaves the living room: only for smashing the singles, not for bathing, not for the albums. He doesn't bath anymore, for a month no water knows the surface of his outer crusts. There is a toilet, off this living room for the singles charts.
He packed his shelves with edibles, non-perishables, ready to eat non-nourishables.
He barely eats.
He is shallow, sallow; like the skinny, yellow sheaves of wheat sprouting inside the sun deprived damp granaries, lacking in character, self-interested, contractive, unintelligible....
He is trapped
He leaves the chessboardalone, unused, on the wasted grey sofa.

He fishes his old Mbira instrument among his stuff on the couch, a warped Nyunganyunga thing. *Mbira music?*Now it has only three out of seven, of its keys left on the upper row. And two middle keys on

15

the lower row. He touches the upper keys with his fingertips, puffs of dust music rose off its gourd inlaid belly, dusty sounds- a strange primitive melody rivers out of the keys, and then he deepens it with the lower two deep keys. He feels, with each touch of the keys, as if he is drawing circles on top of the river's waters.

The forked shadow of music, an echo, a decaying interval, a beginning, a blue shift delayed, as he jumps those empty places were other keys should have.
Her space, in his life, is like those empty places where other keys are supposed to be, creating silent silences, silentmusics.
And when the last note dies, silence rules.
The silence's music finds him shoring up against a loss, a loss that isn't there!
Talking silences? Talking music!
Talking silences, musical silences?

He is dying
He is dying himself, and inside him, he feels that quick, sour blackness, but the greying edges are worn out so finely, that he has got a sinkhole in him that whistles clean.
There is only yesterday and now- tomorrow sneezes in a broken triangular shape whose name he would kill to learn.
There is no outside, only inside
. . . .
Rooms
Looms
Walls
Holes
Mirror
Mirror
. . . .

16

THE WAR

I have decided to leave this city of war. The war has gone out of
control. You never know who belongs to whom,
anymore. What the fight is all about.
The war is still dragging on its
fiery tail through the
dead city like
some
giant prehistoric creature. I take a maze of trail, which threads
its way out of the city, through the unchecked growth
and rubbish. I keep walking, leaving the images
of the city, into the wilderness. The sky
is layers of cotton-thick smoke.
Wild, cross-bred thorny
roses, scraggly
Aloe
plants, hollyhocks, and emaciated chrysanthemums dotes the
trail. Sprigs of tamarisk, sprigs of furze, herbs still
exuding scents, the grass is singing dirges
around my feet, as I pass between
air's legs, it snakes a hiss,
a bark. I begin to see,
to feel another
war
in these species difficult and deeper into great piles of life
fomenting. An irresistible occasion, this garland of
demonstrations! Morning glories, their
purple flowers look down on the
melee much as generals
observe their wars
whilst others
are

17

doing the actual fighting. These generals are the ravishment of
their own extending success, a display. The wheat fields
weaving brushstrokes of their pride, they dance
and shout as of people of a ceaselessly
bombed city when it's freed.
Rose bushes poised
like ballerinas,
a
choreography which gathers them in front of the
forsythia. Quack grass, thistle, cockleburs and
black eyed Susan: are the privates,
sergeants, lieutenants,
and captains;
fighting
the
war for the generals, the morning glories. This war does not
pace itself, space itself..., for it is self-contained in itself

Two Children

I have stayed with a lot of people, over the years, at our place.
And, some day, I was going through old stuff, pictures,
letters, notes... And I see a photo I don't know who
were in the picture, and who left it. It stands
there in my hands like an accursed thing,
an outcast, or a sacrifice to the
unknown spirit. I stare at it,
and still it doesn't bear
any resemblance
to anyone,
to any
of
the people who have shared the place with me, but it must have
been left by any one of the ten or so people or families I have
stayed with. It is the shadow I have always thought is in the
rooms, and a prophet and countless medium spirits said
there were two children in the rooms. I could see the
two children, and the rest of the photo seems
spoiled with dirt, smudgy, moth eaten in
places, and dusty. There is the rich girl,
she is unhappy, and I mean to ask
her why, but I can't ask
her. I don't know
how to talk
to
spiritual beings. She is tanned under a white dress with spaghetti
straps. It's obvious she is bored with herrichness, and then,
there is a poor boy. Guilty?Doubt? Yet it's a face that
echoes that ofa poor child. The two children
gaze onthe camera's foci, bored

becausethey have no idea
whatmelancholy is,
andthe rest
of
thephoto seems spoiled. I have been staring at the spoiled spaces
for some time now, and then I start seeing forms imaging.
I am seeing a baby. I look again, and yes there is a baby,
like images on a dirty window, dusty window panes,
like two children's handprints, as if the baby was
delivering priestly blessings. But, I know this
isn't a pure baby, a pure spirit, that I am
seeing. I realize in my poem's title I
should have included this
baby, this child
who sees,
who
knows, an imp, a little demon (are they the same?), a mischievous
child. This is the baby that has blanketed me with shadows
I didn't know. The baby's arms points to places
in the sky where stars should have been.
His face stands straight up like he
is trying to give the wind
something
to dry its
hands
on.
This
is the
boy who
had turned
into the arms
of a mothering
sleep, in this house

WE WERE MANY

When we were little we were many of us
Half of us left for the sea, a big ocean
Hunger unabated
Half of us found the land
And lived

THE ALTER OF THE DARK

I have red-black lips,
I have red-black teeth,
I have red-black mouth
I have red-black smile
My mouth is full of pain
Eyes drowned in envy,
Ears dripping out ghouls,
Skin fermenting out shit
Spewing out dirty into the sky
Sadistic droppings of scorn

I am crowds, of all nightmares,
dead minds insurrecting
I am a sunken story,
Empty heart, a dry existence
Watered by sewage,
The sewage waters flowing
through my veins, arteries
Like unwritten lines in
An unwritten book

My fate blanks out my flesh;
My blood boils the skeleton in me
Bones into dark blood,
Into nothing, like
Outside looking outside is
Inside looking inside-
nothingness!

The thirst of despair
Overcomes me
With the evil being that is
fomenting inside me
This urge to cling
And cling and cling
On the cracks of the world;
Failure, inferring, uniqueness, interesting

Teardrops, dead waters,
Death's waters, water of the dead,
Dead drops of black blood out of me, dead words
The blood's colour
Is driving nails
Through my heart, deeper and deeper
and deeper and deeper
Into a dance with the devil
To scale the balances of a dark-knight, nighted night

I feel the emptiness
But I can't determine its place, its cause
Only what it is doing to me
It is breaking grounds, breaking hearts; gulfs, revolving
Brilliance, dominance
That is a burden, in their densities, it is difficult to breath

I am a saga, upwind of you
I am downwind of myself
My heart cries out every morning, mourning
With mountains of moans
I am a prisoner of time after sunset, dark nights
A million moans escapes me

As soulless as a tool, or a nail boring into a hole, trying to recall
What I said is my handle

Dreams, Paintings, Light

The skinned
Haloed light
Hello you *light!*
The *light* that sweeps and whispers
Of the birthing room
At Mount MelleryMission Hospital, missing it he remembers it,
when his mother was giving birth to a sister: Katarina. Giving his
sister birth/giving birth to his sister, is the act of giving, giving,
giving...

It's this light; it's this smell...*a light that smells*. He was born there; he
remembers his birth in misremembering it. The memory of which
is like a dream of the backbone in which the backbone rapes its
own memory. Not rape but abuse its memory.

He doesn't like it much, not his birth. He was happy to leave the
room. He knew a *birthing room* is where death and life fights. It's the
fighting that he is always having in his *dreams*, fighting for his life,
his sanity.
He wins the fights by *painting light,*
Painting light; light that is hardly like *light*, it sustains, it illuminates but
it exacts nothing from anyone.

He has been sleepwalking. He has been doing that every night.
Some nights, he would write, some nights he would sing, some

nights he would take his camera and take pictures, some nights he would *paint*, draw figures, sketches on his canvass, inside him. He knows he would be doing all these, when he sleepwalks away from his *fighting dreams*, but he faintly remembers doing: music, visual art, photography. It is nights when he writes and *paints* that he remembers. He finds the manuscripts (canvasses) on his bed, sometimes.

Sometimes they would stay long on his brain, to reproduce them; sometimes he has to use his imagination to reproduce them, the *light* in his imaginations straining and shabby.
He has started *painting*, lately.
He borrowed the *paint* brush from his brother-in-law, to *paint* his house. But he hasn't been able to do that, yet,
He doesn't want to!

During the days, he looks at the brushes and, he knows it's something he wouldn't be doing very soon, *painting* the house. It's his code in the desert he has created, inside himself. He is afraid if he were to *paint* the house, the *painting dreams* would go, and he wouldn't know how to deal with the loss,
Bereft feelings,
The fights,
He has to keep away from it.
It's at night when he uses these brushes.

And this night he started to want to *paint* in his *dreams*. *Painting* is when he finds calm, in his sleep. If he doesn't do one of the art things above, he has to fight the whole night, fighting things he doesn't understand. There are all sorts of battles, sometimes he has to travel, to walk. They are *river dreams*, rivers he will be trying to cross, monsters stopping him.
He had been *dreaming* such a *dream*,

Or is it *re-dreaming* such a *dream?*
He knew, he had had that *dream* before.

He was walking off to somewhere, with a girl, he had been dating, Cynthia. She loves him, she tells him she does, and he sees she tries, but his heart is not in it.
Can one try to love?
Engineering love, or even re-engineering love?
He doesn't know!
How much this woman wanted meaning, but inside him layer upon layer of him was floating.

He has stopped seeing her, it's two times now. When he had this *dream*, he had stopped for the second time.
He would stop again, he knows, before he finds her, before he loses himself in her *light* and shades.
Maybe he is scared of committing to someone, to die into someone. Is that not what love is, dying, to revolve (rapture) between sky and earth? *Boom bang pwaa…*

She is coming, he doesn't know from where, and she is going back to her place. Sometimes, it's like in Chitungwiza where he stays, sometimes it looks like in Johannesburg, where he has stayed. He is talking to her, then she starts moving faster, trying to lose him, but he follows her. They arrive at the place she stays, it's a brothel. She runs into the insides, leaving him outside. At that moment, its deep gutted inside him, how much he wanted her to teach him how to evolve from quivering fins to bursting stars! But, the Guard refuses him entry inside…but someone, a block away, beckons him over. She tells him, the girl is a hooker girl. She shows him a path to use, into this room she has disappeared into. He follows her, he enters the building, and then he realises its empty in the insides!
No house, no rooms, nothing, not her!

26

There is nothing inside but an articulate silence that explains everything,
She has disappeared.

He leaves for home, there is a dam he skirts on his way. There are stepping stones, and he doesn't fall into the waters…he keeps going home. He starts fighting things, some with the intent to kill him, some to waylay him from his path home.
He stays focused…he keeps walking…but he doesn't reach home.
And then, he is returning back.

He doesn't know why he is returning. He didn't find the home, and in his returning, there is something that is still calling him, to go home, but he can't seem to. The way home, there is now this huge river. When he looks at it, he knows he can't cross it. The monsters are inside…so he keeps going, not home.
He is so dead, in his feelings.
He feels the only way to do is to back flip back onto the way home.
He is troubled!

So, he takes the bigger brush…
He starts *painting* the dawn, in the sky he is seeing. There are cracks in the dawn….where there was *light, grey light* comes and swings hard to the left, and they are rain clouds foaming that knits a nest of air and space. And the air crosses clouds in hot nets increasing the local air's tenor uprightness. He has *painted* these rain clouds before. After quiet a long time, in which he is *painting and painting* the sky…there is an opening in the greying skies, or is it considerably less grey. And then, the sky finds its tongue and stutters a few syllables of spring, *lightning light*. The scene has changed abruptly, dramatically, although nothing in his insides has changed.

The dawn is falling away...
It's getting dark on the western sky, though the east...there is the beginning of the coming sun, the *sun's light*. The wind has died down a little and the *light* is more intense in the east, and less and less intense in the west. High up those eastern horizons, the horizon blushes for him, and it's the extraordinary voluptuousness that pervades high places that astonishes him. He is in the middle of such a sky!

The rows of columns of clouds to the west seem to float with their *light capitals*, and their invisible foundations, and he expected, at any moment, to see their delicate shafts breaking up in their moving waves, like reflections in water.

He is in the middle of such a play of *light*.
His soul is flooded with too much *light*.
In the western skies *creviced light* floods, near him into damned places in his insides. And these damned places inside him are holed out arenas, black holes, *lassoed in light*. In the east *new light* flooding in, is miraculous energy, *light diving* in like an eagle, such accuracy and surprise mesmerises him.
It's a sun-kissed benediction.

But, he doesn't feel it's enough for him. The river still calls him-Home calls him. It's like he almost has epiphany, a date with it!
Painting the sky doesn't stop him from wanting to go home...
So, he takes the smaller brush, rubbish brush, *painter's brush*, round brush, brittle unbroken brush, a maker's brush, brushing. The western sky becomes completely hidden by a fast moving cloud of *dark light*, whispering dampness, and the wind is now exhilarating. He tries to *paint* his own portrait, using flaming hues of red passion for his favourite T-shirt, smooth beach water blue for his well-worn shorts, soul brother brown for his rafters, his skin, and double

electric green blended around his portrait, together creating this person.
Is that my head…it looks too big!

His frame is shooting *a bold ray of light* cascading beauty and wisdom. But, still the *light of his dreaming* is not unfurled.
He decides to go home.
He starts moving again, *into his dream…*
He has his two brushes. He knows he could *paint* when it becomes too much for him. There are some people he identifies, because they are friendly, but doesn't know their names.
It's now an extension of *the first dream…*

He has to cross the river. Its muddy, fully flooded. A toe in the water would take him downwards, or into the world of the monsters. He gets to the river's edges, eventually after a long walk. The monster unfurls water as it dives for him. It's a monster shark thing with teeth flung out to gulp him. He avoids its huge blow by a whisker…, as he runs off the river. It splatters heavily, into flesh and blood, blooding the rocky road, just behind him. He doesn't stop to check, he runs off. He knows this one is dead. But, he also knows another is still alive in the water. Suddenly, he reaches some building, and finds shelter there. He tells these people he identifies but do not know their names; that the other monster is on its way. They say they would destroy it. He doesn't wait to see, how. He keeps running, but he is seeing what's happening,
With his behind eyes!
They have created a huge wall.
In his *dream*, he is running but he is seeing the scene.

He stops his mind from running with his body by *painting* again. A *light* in his canvass is like one in which everyone, all those people

who are fighting the monster for him are from another year, not old, not young, but who they were he doesn't know?
He tries, and fails, to make *the play of light* defines these people.

Only that they are now different, enlivened in their task; bright, beautifully bright, *in yellowed light.*
It's like; the *light* is showing him how one person maybe ensouled through the continued experience of others.
Bathed in a light, unreal air, into new clarities...
There is a moon to the south!

The moon licks him with its *shinning mould of lighting speed.* He says, to himself; One day he would be the moon, and stand at someone's window, *shedding light.* He looks at the scene again.
All he sees is the way the *moon's light* reaches and holds the scene together, and everything is now displayed structure, splay structure, lyrical leisure and strange comeuppance.
And then, the monster thing hits the walls, and splatters into blood.
Everyone shouts in joy,
It is dead!

Whilst the bloated sky he had painted, sky-burst its grey wetness into the streets, RAIN, it doesn't matter where; it descends and it follows the curve of the earth. He loves rain
In his soul, he sees himself crossing the river.
He laughs at the moon so hard that it might give up on its stars.
Suddenly everything is alright for him, *in his dreams.* He is on his bed, sleeping.
When he wakes up...
He will wake up from this night, lucid and alive, remembering it all!
He knows he has created a masterpiece, in his head.
This is one canvass he will keep.

TIME #2

Time, like dreams open forgotten realms of creation
Time, like space separates us from events
Time is a torn cloth
Time flogs us with its vicious seasons
Time takes all the time
Time eats time, not us
We don't waste time
Time doesn't waste us
It doesn't waste love
Time can't tell love
Time is
Transitional
It's an object on the move
To enter
I said, inner
Sadly, tenderly
Time might mate
With me

A PORTFOLIO OF DEFIANCE

I am stretching out my wings
Winging away to the mountain of promise, potential
With every right to hope
I am taking this shape, you could shape, too
….it's a saying, or is it musical?
I need to survive the thunderstorms and be a new rose
Spewing perfume, blooming…
With every right to hope

The fires are still doing, negotiating
With black veins stuffed with hope
Dreams, angers; a soul
Of undeterred definitions of scope

No clocks, I know what time it is
The manure pilled around my bones, one day
Will become the garden that I ought to be
But in the meanwhile I put in the work and dreamed I will succeed

I have clenched a coal hot October sun in my being; carry it in my throat,
dry, accumulating pain, hot, burnt
Want of a horizon of water, knowing it would boil me
A pocket of it might do, maybe moistening me
Maybe, I will pour out a steaming pot, steeped with smoldering of positivity

I weave constellations (galaxies that think rhapsody) from memory,
the Milky Way blued into the loom with fainting threads
I burn the stars with my cold breath, the swooshing, steaming
sounds of burnt stones, immersed in water

I have found threads of meaning in this existence
Ropes without meaning
I have opened out these threads, with my mouth
I have tied everything to these threads, unthreading the ropes,
everything
All at once

I incline towards complexity spaced seriality of life units
I will be the tallest person on top of the mountain
The grown up

A bird with its river flows
The bird, breaking the sky, effortlessly
The lark's amplitude, disintensive
Up and up it feels, it says it is free
O, ohohoh, I am the lark, ohohoh
In my intensive disintensiveness
My brain humming with infrasonic success

Old man, Dreams, Writing

We had had some words with the old man,
    in the afternoons. He stays in Felicia Street, number 9,
and I stay in Douglas Road, number 9, so our places
are opposite each other, opposing each other like polar points,
dissonance, like synchrony
It's an upper middle class suburb;
Birchleigh North, in Kempton Park, Johannesburg.
This old man I am writing about, in my dreams, is a prickle old
thing, complaining at the slightest raise of any volume. He sits on
his veranda that overlooks our backyard, where we are supposed to
play, but we can't make noise. Its midday, and he has tea, a big cup,
clay cup and a plate of biscuits, I think, store bought ones…and he
is happy. A beam of sunlight hits the top of his bald head, like a
penlight flicking on. I am writing; I stare at what I have written
about him. Did I show you, so far, that I don't like him? I am not
saying I don't like him. But, I am writing
that I don't like him. Are they the same? Let me check the page. I
stare at
the page , at most precisely, the space an inch to the left of my ball
point pen, an Eversharp pen- looking for a word, a phrase, a
thought, that is trying to jump out of the sentences,
that is trying to make you have sympathy on this old man
Some things don't just change…I have been using an Eversharp
pen
for over thirty years, since my grade school, and there was a Bic
pen. Bic died,
did it, and Eversharp stayed Eversharp and I am still using an
Eversharp pen.
And if I am ever sharp I can prod spatial pleasure from the texture,

34

textiness of this text, whilst the intellect
in you is confounded. I gaze as if these words might feel
my gaze, like a slight breeze, and behave well. I
want this writing to be the rope I will follow from this dark forest
slip of dreams, in these severe and
relentless thunderstones, to the Ellesey Suburb, so that
I might feed with all the others there.
I want the old man to behave, as well. But
would you tell someone that old to do that
Not him. Unless if you want to write it, his answers, a column of
ten…soldiers
arranged for an invasion, battle of Normandy for you
…. *you!*

                  …. *you!*

                                  …. *you!*

….. *you!*

                  …. *you!*

                                  …. *you!*

…. *you!*

                  …. *you!*

                                  …. *you!*

…. *you!*

…. you, and he will continue calling
you, …. you. You
would almost think, it's now your name, as he goes inside
to the phone, to call the police. I stayed with
my brother at this place,
so he was having a party for his little kid who had turned
1, and he had invited
his friends over.
I didn't know how others were doing but I,
personally, I was getting tanked.

It was George, his vulgar friend who matched this old man.
Replying every of his .... you with an equally fucked up .... you of
his own. And the whole party crowd joined in, calling the old man,
....*you*,
.... *you*,
old faggot .... *you*,
everything became .... *you*,
the party was .... *you*,
Douglas Road became .... *you*,
Birchleigh north .... *you*,
I never really liked the place. It was too white.
We were the only black family in that street.
And fucking enclosed with electrified barricades,
and only one gate
out of it.
If you wanted to go to two streets down us,
which was outside the barricades,
you would have to go up 8 streets to the exit point,
and then take Straydom Road,
down 11 streets to Pangolin drive, which is just
two streets from Douglas Road
The place was an island, curved out for the protection of one race.
The neighbours, who were white, also entered in, calling us
.... *you*
The police came and called everyone at the party,
.... *you*.
This situation was feeding backwards and forwards, running ahead
of myself, and then rolling
off this pen. Like the barking of dogs, I have just gone out of our
gate, and suddenly;
it is dogs, dogs, dogs, as I go up to the gates. Black hair, of mine,
spiking up like stalactites

It's the noise of dogs barking, wanting to eat me. It's the Whiteman's dogs that are the vessels of the white man's dislike of a black person;
even black dogs don't like my colour. But they are black, like me.
I see a white guy coming up ahead of me, and there is silence his side of the road, and when I pass him, the side of the road I have left is now silent, and his, which I now plod in,
is dogs, dogs, dogs.
Like these dogs,
the policemen,
mostly black policemen,
took everyone at the party to the
    police station.
    We fucked up in
    the police cells that night.
    We had to bribe them off,
for them to let us the …. out of the cells.
The old man didn't get out
of his house for a fucking long time.
Scarred like shit he became fucking polite afterwards,
sometimes joining us in our fucking noise.
We dealt with a lot of fucking curses
fromour neighbours. We fucking didn't care.
It's supposed to be a fucking
free country.
Oh! It's because I had taken my sight off from the writing that I have been swearing, to stare at the clouds outside the window, to the north, around Ellesey Park, just off Pangolin River, just off Pangolin road, just off this place I liked. It colouredWell.

The clouds looks like burnt clay, were besieging the black, burnt out walls of the northern sky's fringes, as if the clouds were descending to rebuilt this sky. I had been watching that sky, hardly noticing the swear words I had been writing, hardly noticing the change of light around me, as night was becoming morning.

I think to look at my words again. It is a superhuman effort to make my eyes focus on the pen again. It is a dream hare on quicksilver feet, the way my pen is creating mountains and conquering them in its writings, creating oceans and swimming across shark infested oceans, typhoons, hurricanes, tsunamis…all that. I look again at the sky, where they might have been this view; lost space, lost words, long into the woods

And then, the face of that old man slipped back through the window I had forgotten to unlock when I was watching the northern skies, and he tells me, or possibly, I think he tells me, that, it was him, that old man who lives at the house across ours. I know that! That was the old man who was waiting for his beard, purplish whitish as a branch of rowanberries, to grow down into the ground, and root himself to the dead.

I tell him that…or he tells me that. Someone must have told him that in the fight, that night of partying. My gaze focuses on the words I have just written. It never strays from the spot at which the pen has just moved away, the complete line finished, the stanza, perhaps a poem.

Although the old man was as solitary as a finger,
a dream deep inside him warmed him.
His head is a skull; one could see
the shapes of the bones. I want to know his name. I ask him
what his name was, is. He keeps silent, but he is looking
at me with a look that is a name,
which is his name. I see it in
his eyes, and I know it is in my eyes, too.

With my hand still holding
the pen, I stain to hear the old man.
My pen is firmly on the paper, on this page, the old man's voice is
in the sound and smell of the pen's ink, the scratchy sounds the pen
is making as it scribbles the paper,
like whispers on paper, like sheet music,
like a ghost.
He is dead;

it's actually his skull I am seeing.
He has been dead for two years now,
he tells me.

I had left Kempton Park 5 years ago for another city in
Johannesburg, and later for home. That's where I am, home, in
Chitungwiza, writing about this old man. And, I had been thinking
he was still alive, but no. He has been dead for over two years

I ask him where his families are. He tells me he was the only son,
his parents were long since dead when I met him, and he had never
married.
My mind agrees with him.
All the months I stayed in Douglas Road,
I never saw anyone, family; coming to see him.
Then, I thought, he just didn't go with crowds,
but now I realise the truth.

I ask him again what his name was.
I hear my voice in his replies.
He answers me in my own voice
He is me.

A strange chain of associations sweeps me into a crowded maze of recollections, and then, prompted by a faded memory lodged in there, leads me to an irresistible curiosity, but then, my words sets me free...

Maybe it's my writing, that's less clear to you, a handwriting of the Eversharp pen, not my thoughts. Or, I must be undecipherable, me, Hildegard? He is me in these trenches of my schizophonic (not schizophrenic) mind. I am staring at the sharp serrated stones of my life's story.

I wail!

                    I howl!

A voice of blue that shoos the clouds,

                                     I mourn!

I cry!

How nice to notice myself amid this half-conscious offer!

I take my skull which is on his shoulders, and put it on the head that was not mine. It fits in like a self-container (inner self) that springs on this page, and then I am walking off... I don't know where to.

The morning star hangs over the Birchleigh north area, like a drop of blood, giving out so much darkness, yet producing startling light. I am going to the home of an elderly lady who was my first girlfriend, who had hurt me long, long ago. I reach Glenmarias Cemetery at the hour of witches, three AM. Every wave of the wind, an ally, I find her place on the soil, the land mounded (by death's carnival ride) and ragged, undirected, voluptuous strict.

In the trees, the sitter-hum of night birds formations. A bird flies overhead, between the mangy crescent moon, and my left cheek. I

hug her mound, I cry out the waters. She now lies on this ground,
stripped into the ground, into the soil, unraveling sutures,
as lonely as I am now!

CATHEDRAL OF DETOURS

Fighting on the shores of; the soul, memories, Beingness
Trying to escape angular poverty; empty books, brooks, shelves, she lives in
In subordination levels, hammering into the soul, such soul sinking oppression
The poet in her, she stinks to the moon and back
Floating her dreams in the vast deep
At her own beck and call

Poetry being her only religion, playing a dirge, the dirge a sacrament
More than wine changed into water or water into wine
Or the fish swallows Jonah, Jonah swallows the fish
It's a jungle of minds, her insides
Walking dead on streets, empty streets too real for dreaming

Her eyes can see nothing anymore, only the wind
Unhurricaned wind, wild
The "too" soon of tearing, the wind parting the drapes of her mind
The wind, air's chthonic suction, plenary in volume, rambunctious in voice
Black, tickling leaves, rustling, muslin

She is a life painted by chaos
Her future is painted in a lead colour
Painting asking for a second, seconding, opinion
Screaming in the storm
Like lost beauty, the beauty she had, screaming
Bottles and pills, screaming for freedom from her

Her brain matter is suffocating the space within the walls
In the prisons of her mind

Heartache flows inside her, beaten thick with despair
So sweet the despair, so good like stolen food would taste
Drowned in the depths of a cesspool
That she has created, liturgical lock nobody will unlock for her
This ocean of despair is all too consuming

It's kind of a zone
Blood zone, life zone, knowledge zone, grinding zone
Danger zone, separate zones, gaps sewed together
With strings zones
Life's pendulum swinging between the two zones
Life and death's zones

Death, to be stoned, it's a charming death for her
Let the poet in her be stoned, she tells them, in her acidic liturgy
The needle is always too closer to my eyes
And my mind is frozen, soaked in fearful, tearful memories
I am a mind-damaged casualty
Recollections only, of feelings
As I journey into the blended earth.

SANDS OF TIME:
This is my house

Think, think of massive, vast deep sands, those in North Africa,
and I am finding my way in these sands. Somewhere in Morocco,
not in Casablanca, not...   even in the movie. Think of the
ocean of sands, the heat, the hotness, inhospitable, as I travel
to the sea, to the rock Atlantic stuns, to get cooled in Moroccan
currents in   the Atlantic.
I see a bird, maybe a desert crow. I eye the
crow for potential, and it eyes me back. A crow
caught in the act of flying off the
desert's smiles, the desert
lends its voice to the
dead; Inhalations'
monophony and echo, blade.
I have been to a beach before, some-
where, where the warm water (the soul
is lukewarm like the heart of someone fleshly dead)
of the Indian Ocean, and the cold water of the Atlantic meets,
somewhere on the Cape coast. I am now made to think how that
doesn't compare with the sands of this desert. The calm in this
desert   is such that the sands can
be heard groaning beneath its own weight. Hot, I am-
I am chopping into the sands with my blistered feet. I think of the
sand fields, the sand   roads, the river's beaches, sand and
sand I have travelled to wherever whilst the child in me watches,
wonders in memory's house. But this sand I am seeing is enormous
amount of sand; it's sun soaked,   smug and expanse, as
I reach the beach. The beach finds me pixilated and wanting.
But I know the beach's weight will dissolve these clenched
thoughts. Looking   back at the

44

desert, there is sand and sand, and as my sight
grows distant to the point where the sky fingers the
land, it is revealed, reveling, no doubt,
the human…a tiny human out
there. The human; in the
arcade of bones
and joints,
going
outside, away
from the beach,
renouncing mathematics,
single mindedly developing his own
meaning. The result is more like an eye socket
laughing meaninglessly above a set of kneecaps, or nerves
forming up in order to dream. The set of kneecaps speaking to
each other eloquently of a need to collect, to fill time's spaces with
a file of memories,   each one a marker signaling
across loneliness. The flesh is sand; the flesh is dry as you go far
away from the water. The soul is water. The beach is when the
flesh and spirit just makes it. Like   when nature is clothed
in thought! But, the two are at cross purpose most of the time,
each fighting the other by walking off its own existence. The soul
into   a region immersed
in water, and the flesh in a region
inundated by sand. The sand only feels good where
it meets the water, it is at that ever shifting
thin line of the beach, and the
two are at ease with the other.
This line shifts as the flesh
and soul fights
everyday. The
soul needs
a house; it needs

the sands, just like the ocean needs
the sands (the land) for it to be an ocean, without
which it would flood everything in too much soul, like
there is such a thing as too much goodness. The beach is the line
of control, and at that point of control, the sand gives off scent in
confusion.   Like all things human,
animal, I was hungrily made- a blank hole of a thing, gaping,
arching,   which grows, me growing, wide and then
wider like a south that never fails to be struck opus of   being.
Separately the soul and flesh views a demonstration of itself to
uphold a complex melody, the more one moves away from the
beach, and thus, abruptly, it is no longer a soul or flesh. It is the
world   itself, so various, so as not to be spared as it is, as it
were, the impetus never to leave it.

STATIONS OF THE CROSS

He is hitting my head, I am falling to the ground, and he is hitting me, again and again. He is grabbing my hair. He is pounding my head on the floor. He is shouting at me, scolding me, calling me "stupid", "dumb". He is pulling down my skirt and pant. He is taking off his belt, and pulling it into a loop. He is whipping me. He keeps whipping me. I feel like fire is shooting through my body...It hurts to sit for days. A week later, I am going into the church. There is no one in the church, but me. It is quite. It smells good- incense and candles burning. It is so peaceful. I walk over to the Stations of the Cross. I love Jesus. I think I know how he felt...at least a little. I cry. I feel very close to him.

1

The first station of the cross, "Jesus is condemned to death". My father keeps telling me he will kill me, even for small things like changing the channel of the TV

This poem is for those who violate the conventions of human dignity
This poem is for those who violate the conventions of human freedom
This poem is for those who have cut budgets, closed schools
This poem is for Jonah who can't read and write
This poem is for Mathew who is deaf
This poem is for Maria who is blind
They taunted, tormented and teased them
It is a hate crime, the beast that never perished
It re-arranged into these cruel children's hearts
This poem is for children living in child labor camps
Farm boys, hands throbbing from the suns

Working the fields, with no school to go.
Because they are poor, because they are young
Brushing out the lamp of hope in their hearts.
This poem is for children who don't have food, shelter and hope
The weeping child, anguished cries that makes no sound at all
It is for children who know the deep throbbing vacancy of hunger
For food, home, love, space, light and stars that remember.

2

The second station of the cross, "Jesus bears his cross". I feel a heavy weight pressing me down….my father's presence alone in the house is a heavy cross for me.

At 10 days of age, I was shocked by the gunshots of my parents' voices, shouting at each other
At 10 weeks of age, Calvin was fed with Sadza and Mutowejongwe, cock's soup
At 10 months of age, Mary was raped by her father to gain good luck
At 10 years of age, Jane was raped for the third time by our Maths teacher
Is God such a violent man?

3

The third station of the cross, "Jesus falls for the first time". When my father beats me I fall to the ground. He uses his whip until the blood flows.

Since age 11, Jane was refused schooling more than 11 times. Since age 11, Mary was used as a call girl more than 11 times. Since age 11, Jane was given in marriages, treated for sexually transmitted diseases. Since age 11, I was beaten more than 11 times. Since age 11, Mary was jailed in a juvenile facility. Since age 11, Jane was abducted, sold off to Angolan free labour workplaces. Since age 11, Mary was sold off to South African brothels. At age sixteen they were used up. They were just nothing, but a shell. They were released. They found their way home. They are now commercial sex workers. They are fallen angels, fallen down… Down…down, on their crosses.

4

The fourth station of the cross, "Jesus meets his mother". Once father beat my mother when she tried to refrain him from beating me, and now, she only watches- afraid of my father, or she doesn't love me anymore. Cruelty is like a flu bug, it is easily passed around

This poems is for the pregnant girl with nowhere to go
This poem is for the boy in a cruel gang, learning the cruel nature of the world
This poem is for the child trying to make do in life
This poem is for the student called "stupid' who struggles in school
I see every day the increase of young beggars
I see every day the increase of illiterate children
I see every day the increase of unemployable young people
This poem is to kindle a flame of compassion

5

The fifth station of the cross, "Jesus is helped by Simon of Cyrene". I don't have friends anymore. I drive them away because I am always sad

This poem is for the raped girl trying to rebuild her life

This poems is for the teenage girl who is worried she isn't "pretty"
enough
This poem is for the girl who hangs herself because of cruel words
of others
This poem is for the teenage boy who lies about having sex and
doing drugs
This poem should give you courage and hope to carry your cross
This poem is from God
This poem is for you

6

The sixth station of the cross, "Veronica wiping blood from the
face of Jesus". No one wipes my tears for me, I am alone. Only
God wipes my own tears for me.

God is for the ones terrified that this might be all there is in life
God is for the ones who woke up every morning without hope
God is for the ones who wants nothing more than to be loved
God is for the ones who wonder whether they want to continue
living God is for the ones living this life alone
God is for you.
This poem is for you

7

The seventh station of the cross, "Jesus falls down for the second
time. There is a day I thought he had finished beating me. I tried to
rise up and run, but he started beating me again, I fell down again

God is for those who lost the light at the end of their tunnels
God is for those who have pushed far beyond their breaking point
God is for those broken beyond repair

God is for those suffering silently in the dark
God is for those fallen down for the second time
God is for those whose screams no one hears

8

The eighth station of the cross, "Jesus speaks to the women". My bed and I talk about father. We call him the devil. Sometimes we lean against the door while the devil is beating on the door, trying to get to me

This poem is for the ones who realizes not everything is their fault
This poem is for the ones who want to change the world
This poem is for the ones who imagine for a better world
This poem is for the ones who sees hope where most people do not
This poem is for the ones whose minds are opened up by God

9

The ninth station of the cross, "Jesus falls down for a third time". After father beat me down, back on the floor, for the second time, I tried to get up, but I couldn't. I hurt too much and I fell back down for the third time

This poem is for the child of divorced parents who would always struggle
This poem is for the abused child who can never lead normal life
This poems is for the missing child who will never be found
This poem is for broken families whose pain is beyond comprehension
This poem falls down for the third time with you

This poem is for you

10

The tenth station of the cross, "Jesus is stripped of his garments".
Daddy pulls my pants down to whip me

This poem is for the boy who feels striped by bullying at the
playgrounds
This poem is for the child who plays video games all day
This poem is for the youths whose mind is corrupted by
Hollywood and media
This poem is for the girl who only models because she thinks her
body is all she has of value
This poem is for the child who has nothing to value in life
This poem is for those children who feel naked in their souls
This poem is for you

11

The eleventh station of the cross, "Jesus is nailed to the cross".
When I am around father I feel frozen. I feel like I am nailed with
invisible nails to an invisible cross. When he beats me, the whip is
like the hammer hitting at the nails, the whip connecting to my
body is the nail. I can hear it sounding off "gong, gong, gong", on
my flesh. I can feel the pain, hitting the bottoms of my soul. I bled
tears of blood from my soul. I feel myself dying, slowly.

12

The twelfth station of the cross, "Jesus dies on the cross". Father
hurts me. I can't get away. I don't talk to anyone; I am dying inside
my soul.

This poem is for tears no one hears
This poem is for voices lost in this translation
This poem is for voices that die in this translation

13

The thirteenth station of the cross, "Jesus is removed from the cross". When I remained on the ground, father yanked me off the floor, holding my hair. He dumped me on my bed, but I couldn't sit. My body is all wounds. I can't even rise myself, as he rapes me. I am powerless. I am dead.

14

The fourteenth station of the cross, "Jesus is buried". I am buried in a grave, I know. Like Jesus, I am a seed; I know one day I will leave it all. One day, I will reach the end of my tunnel.

This poem is for those waiting for a better tomorrow
This poem is saying we are all one in God
This poem is saying love is all we really need
This poem is saying, "Stop child abuse!"
This poem is for Mathew
This poem is for Calvin
This poem is for Jane
This poem is for Mary
This poem is for Maria
This poem is for Jonah
This poem is for you
And you
And you
And you...

PLACE OF LOVE

If his heart was reliant on the outside world then what primal
materials would make up this reliance
Her heart is a weave of charcoal, blue spruce, hymns, incense,
Spider's silk; materials hardly seen as fortress
Their love, and the hallows that live within it is best housed in a
loose weave
Like woods would feel best when it is raining, barely raining...

The green leaves of trees in the rain fluttering and sneezing in
happiness
A life-throb of ages dancing, in the rain
Is love's low cascade, a decade in a bird's eyes
As evening flows in and around them
It's a life that shoots in joy through the dirty of the earth

Sometimes her hands, in panicky, all over him
If he can nestle into her palms
He sighs up like a turtle dove
As he coves her, the secret places between them
Their lovemaking; it is life, it is the sky falling where only love can
go
It is a desire that embraces the margins
They are fumbling on love as they are stuck in the shock of it

The graph of love is like the place of space
The graph of space is like the place of love
She is on top of the mountain; she looks up at the wonderful sky
The sun beams on her beauty

She waves down at those who look up to her, at him

Obviously its possibilities, obviously everywhere, obviously feeding
their humming spheres
With the music of each other's names
Admitting how spasmodic their bodies are
Beyond the given over music of orgasm
Twirls in, *good morning, I love you.*

There are, in their soft containers
They are rough, rapid and ready
To figure out each other, to figure out love
And, when their bodies are orientated
Satisfaction with the surroundings is almost psychical as swimming
in no wind

He watches her jack hammering notes into her memory
At the curious inward look people would have, that's in her eyes
When they have not yet formed a face they will wear to look out on
the world
The breathlessness of that moment, small, wondrous
And, the only noise is made by their hearts beating
Silence yoking love's toll

She sleeps with him, to speak to the ape whose hibernation
habours humanity
Teaching each other about the strings, which makes things strings?
That fray and tangle
Turning on curiosity as a passkey
Their longing equals each other's longings

She is not just his friend; she is his heart, himself
For him, life was a bed, a window, a friend come visiting

Before he met her
He is now of father and mother
She is the father and mother
Like water, it is love

Allowing their hearts no hindrance even when they are silent
They still sound each other's smells in secret
Which was always heart's home?
What is pain?
What is really pain in this place of love?

****

*The things that keep them menacing enough in the face of what aims
to name them menacing things, menacing meat, menacing animals, menacing
each other?*

THE HYENA IN ME

I fix myself to attributes unknown   of a howling invisible
absence
Whittling away at the   shadow of this
moment's utterance
Labels are for   the eyes of the lucid,   whereas
the mouth is   patently sharp
I see idols   without   identities in
the etymology   of faith, epiphanies migrating
like   fins
flying
Flying away   on wings, like dust   motes
floating, like   microscopic seraphim, in the sun
seeping through the   windows. Like hollowed   spaces
lifting off the broken   meteor-hearted crates

In a Shona parable, I am   the hyena that deals with several
stumbling obstacles;   each one involves meat, because the
hyena in me loves meat.   It adores meat like the bear adores
pears. The hyena in me   starts on its journey to prove that it can
triumph over   any temptation put in its path. It sees dead
carcasses of eagles,   buffalo, cows, lions…, but it triumphs. It
doesn't eat   them. It has passed through every other meat
animal,   it has passed through geese gathered like
contrabassoons   by the lake, and every time it triumphs, it
sings its   song of triumph

Temptations call for me, who I would stand with, I will stand by my God

It walks for nights, years   and years, and it is now an old
hyena, with a lifetime   hunger (deep inside of it) of meat.
And, after a lifetime of it;   eating grass and fruits, and as it was

about to enter its   heaven, it finds the carcass of a wild hog,
sizzling fat,   decaying a bit with such a smell, in the burning
afternoon   suns. The smell stokes its hunger.
It kills the hyena!

This smell indicates   the hyena in me, as a   place of
good soil   begets an abundance of colours; the colours
of healthy, and of forms.   And, one wonders   whether
this demonstration will   be able to walk off this itself,
maybe later, or if it   will feel inclined to toll in the meat, the
music   in its heaven or in its hell
But, for the parable,   this demonstration holds   its
instrument musical,   wavering before it topples into inversion,
into melodic complexity.

i AM Going TO Marry HER

A boy, who thinks he is a man, and a woman who thinks she is a girl. One in Harare, the other is in Johannesburg. He is Oedipus. He is like Oedipus. Oedipus is like Chaka Zulu. She is MbuyaNehanda. Chaka Zulu is like Mzilikazi. MbuyaNehanda is a man, like say, Tichakunda. Why didn't you marry all these years? You are now 40. 40 is like the new 30, 30 is like 20, 20 is like 0, the new 0. We get born at 20, yet some say life begins at 40. Bit by bit this ageing is the prey, he will feast on it. Zero is like a hero, at that hill. I was waiting until I mature, I was pursuing something else, and that is nothing. Nothing is something which is nothing. Iteration, and you are asking me what's going to happen, and I am saying it's already happening, like silent things talking in the dark. Mzilikazi is like king Makoni. Whose head, or is it skull, or whatever is somewhere like not here, somewhere like No(r)where(way). They took his brain to learn about how an intelligent African man thinks. He had made his own Chimurenga from his bode of Makoni, and they didn't know what genius drove this war thinker. Tichakunda is her boyfriend, her lover, and she has been trying to figure out how he functions, taking his brains into her heart. With heat she hopes to change her luck lustre, halt the continuing built of years on his frame. I am single and I have told her I love her when she was a burning thing on me, Tichakunda thinks, King Makoni is Lobengula's lover. The first job Lobengula had was taking down his pants and pee to an old man in Matopos hills, who lived near Rhodes' gravesite. It was easy money, steady work, and flexible hours. The old man never touched Lobengula, never frightened him. He just gave him money, a dime for every puddle he made. Lobengula was a boy, in the shadows of his father Mzilikazi. And they say it's a western invention. Lobengula watched the Matopos sands turn dark as the hot liquid (puddle) spread. It felt good, very liberating, and he got his dime (to

59

buy sugar), and he accepted it, and kept it as a secret, between him and the old man. Lobengula is like Nkomo (which one, it's not a question.), Nkomo is like Mugabe (Davidsons) David's sons is like Z, is like MbuyaNehanda, MbuyaNchanda who is like Winnie Mandela. Winnie Mandela is like Mitchell Obama, and is that African. Osama is like Obama (not Winnie Obama). So, you are now ready to marry (me). Winnie asks Nelson, Nelson who is like Desmond. Desmond is like Robert. Robert is like Helen. Helen is my grandmother. Yes, I am now ready to marry (you) grandmother. Helen is happy, her drapes open up. Helen tells the good news bible to her AU-ntie Joyce. Joyce is happy. She is going to pick a fat cheque (Auntie's dowry). Joyce is like Joseph, the goat's face is like Pumzile, who is like Simon. Simon is like Thabo, who is like Jacob, who is like Cain, where the hell is that son of mine; I can feel he is trouble. Jacob is like Joshua (tree), like John, like Didymus, like Kgalema, like Emerson, like Morgan. Morgan is like Tendai, not me. I am like Tichakunda. I am going to marry her. And they offered him a scholarship to write a bio note about Davidsons. Does Davidsons work at ZESA, ZIMSEC, ZIMRA, ZEC, ZISCO, and Z…LAST? And they denied me my chance to write about (a novel, which is poetry) South Africa, 60 plus million years ago. They say they know everything from back then. I could have told them they don't know because they don't speak the language anymore. It was the world before voice, before the ape in you. Maybe I should have proposed to write this poem about Tichakunda and his girl Nehanda. I am listening to her favourite music, singer, Tracy Chapman, *across the lines…*, and who doesn't like Tracy. Tracy is a pickpocket. Tracy is like Celine, who is like Dolly, the sheep, who is like Whitney, who is like Bobby, Mariah, who is like Madonna…not the painting from that mad painter. It's Picasso rather who painted it, so a kid could have painted it. But who doesn't like a bio note on Picasso, who is like Madonna, who is like Celine. But they are not African. African as Africa is for

Africans, ask Davidsons. So what is Irene doing here? She told me I don't have talent. She said I am like Mbidzo, Mbidzo who is like Tsitsi, who is like Batsi, who is like Charles, who is like the-far-way, who is like Christopher, who is like Dambudzo, who is like Shimmer, shimmering in the morning's sun like dew would. Mbidzo rhymes rhythmically, poetrically. But, I don't. Is this a poem? Irene whatever, whatever Irene, I mean whatever. Irene is right, which is correct, that I don't have talent. So, they were correct, which is right in giving him the scholarship to write about Davidsons who is Z, is like Z. I am the last one of my group at school to want to marry, so I must not have any talent, even for marriage. I will be the last one to marry. I have succeeded without talent, to even make someone think of it, to think of it, myself, me, I. At last, this time they did not recycle the winners, they vary in subtle, unimportant ways. It's getting such that it's a monarchy system, feudatory, with its masters and servants and sycophants, and prescription (proscription, the dictionary says they are different) writing. This pork barrel pedagogy they are peddling is like selling a blanket bearing measles. Those who were the selectors, as like always, are from the same crowd, who win prizes but do not publish books afterwards, or if they publish, it's always one book wonder...and they are so talented. At least 4 were not from the same country. I would rather (if they were going to be 4 winners) they would have come from South Africa this time. Me, Tichakunda, because I am HERE (go and debate this if you want) is included with my thesis on South Africa before voice, which is word...and I won't write in these words, in this voice, and the next one should have been Julius (a star sized mind of a moon sized man, knowing that he has a lot to say) with his apartheid diatribe South Africa, this and that, the next one would be Mongosuthu on Nelson's bio note, and Nelson would write Desmond's bio note. It's already sold out man! They are always messing us here, messing us there, trying to rectify here, messing that, rectifying this,

61

rectifying that. The rectification is complete on our loyal disaffection. Let me write a bio note about them. Me and the 253 who were messed in June, me and the 100 plus messed in July, me and the 300 plus messed in November, that is December. Me. Me. Me, that is always like me, me, and me. I am going to marry her, to love her concretely. Today I almost wrote a sentence! Z is like Z, which is like ABC, which is like XYZ, and I can't unhappen what has happened. I am always caught in this cycle of losing, and this is a curtained caterwaul. Now, I feel better.

VOICES

Knock: strike a surface noisily to attract attention, collide with, strike, strike, strike someone or something so that they would move, move, move and/or fall. We knock on the doors with bended fingers: knock, knock, knock.... *Gogogoi, may we come in please;* we say as we come into your heath. This is followed by a pause, a pregnant pause, the right pause, waiting for your answer. It's a voice wanting to come out, knocking in, to come in, in, in...
We knock upon silence for an answering voice
What if knocking could answer itself--- knocking

Voices are sounds produced by the person's larynx and blown out through mouth, a speech or song, ability to speak or sing, *hmmmmm, do so mi re dot do far mi mi re do...,* the range or pitch or type of tone with which a person sings *wuuuuuuuu.* It is a voice as speech or song; sing, sing, she sings a storm, dances. There are other voices like grunts*himm,* cries *yuwii,* clucks *tshack,* sighs *uhuuu,* bird's voices, tame that cicada, please! Of the wagging laughter of water in Nyajezi River. Or the sounds of Madasanana creek's water over flat stones, sounds like people talking and laughing, kind of creepy voice. And, it's the voice of Nyangombe River when it is flooded that has the biggest voice...it's a droning voice, little music...it's like anger. These are voices that talks, even a lot louder than voices as speech and song. Anger can talk, too; when we think it is the soul that's talking. Voices are like a stethoscope detecting seismic vibrations, collecting, trigonometrically confusing, and calculating. Talk that calculates, calculates, calculates itself to zero, negatives...
A voice that talks
...are there voices that do not talk. It's not a question! Neither an answer...
We talk upon silence for an answering voice

63

What if talking could answer itself--- talking

To talk is to speak in order to give information (what of talk that doesn't give information) mumbling, mumbling, rumbling, rummaging around speech, or to express ideas or feelings, to be able to speak, speak, speak, I shall not speak, a speech, voices, to discuss something thorough. Thoroughly cleaning the classrooms of thought whilst talking, talking, talking, like we used to clean those classrooms at school, aghhh... I am utterly fond of talking, telling. Talk to me, please! He will talk your head off. We need to talk. Well, do you want to see my back, talk to my back? We want to be silent some other time. Fasting; from talking, silently...
We are silent upon silence for an answering voice
What if silence could answer itself--- silence

Silence as complete lack of sound *mwiii*, voice *shiiii*, speech *nwiiii*, talk, a situation in which someone is unwilling to speak, I won't speak of..., discuss something, silences, silencing, silencer... Puutuuuuu... the sounds of the revolver spouting out bullets...it's like her silences to me. It talks. When there is no voice: are we silent: death, die, dead...

Unsettled things scatter around like autumnal leaves in the wind, float, whimsies...
Like sentences coming undone in:
Syllables drifting to the surface
Vowels bowling down to the bottom, bottoming
Consonants constantly going up and down
To the surface of the ocean, off the ocean's surface
Our voices are our father's voices

Our voice is the choice that we are
It is what we want to do, what we do not want to do,

64

With our lives, with other people's lives.
What do you want to do with me, my life, my lives?
Our voice purposes as a commentary
Our voice is ownership and autonomy
Commentary on Ownership and Autonomy:
Broadcasting (commentary as in sports casting), explaining,
expressing; belonging (ownership of one's voice), possession: our
own goal (autonomy), own goal. Jam Stap, stamping a ball past
Peter Sch(smile)micheal, self-governing Dutch overseas territories
into an own goal, that is, Greenland is to Denmark. Manchester
United…Man Uuuuuu, late 90s, early 2000s
A voice, in football terms!
Striding past all that all could be

In it we find, invisible forces of new words, invisible
Forces of words that are in a new space, places, times
Not Times Square!
It takes full control over-
Control, controlling, controlled, directing, limiting, regulating.
Managing? Nikki.
Do you believe Nicki Manager; Minaj-ing, is talking the music
world into a machine fantasy, is an ocean without water, talking,
talking, talking…. On top of this empty ocean cruise ships, like
Tom Cruise, a monster ship, titanic, titaniking somewhere in the
North Sea, harvesting seaweed for his friend, a girl Katy, Perry?

It's just patterns of language, it creates
A voice that comes from, is
Demanding, pressing, paradoxical
Don't run to the dictionary:
It's a statement that sounds absurd, or seems to contradict, itself.
The dictionary will even contradict you, but may in fact be true; a
person or thing that combines contradictory qualities, androgyny.

Robert Duncan, on his poetical pedestal, knowing how to take advantage of androgyny and mood swings, saying, ….*Thus, in actual world, the world as we call it, men "found" or founded signs of God (voices (of)for God), perceived and believed, and in this realized, that this being was all, and that one's own existence was but part among such a multitude, inconceivable, of parts in the universe of that being, coexisting through time and space as Eternity, that self existed only in terms of that Being.*
The real world, the world we know, the world we inhabit,
is God, is us, in our multiplicity,
is the being, is the universe.
Where the hell is hell, then?
Duncan, where the heaven is heaven?
Us? Yet, he is right!

It is the presence of duende
Not Paula duende, in a song, its De Anda?
"Walk away", "Walk away", "Walk away."
Sweetness accruing sweetness, telling you to walk away
From the beauty, from her voice
It's not easy to walk away from beauty
It's the inexplicable transfixing
Qualities, evident in her voice, in beauty
That gives us that feeling, chills
Mysterious, profoundly, this feeling?
I can't even explain it, as you can see!

Are voices there for us to hear what's not there?
Are voices there for us to hear what's not there?
Did I repeat myself?
So, where there are no words
Don't we hear?
"Hear me, oh Lord",*Oliver Mtukudzi* belting out his plea to the Lord.
It's Oliver Mtukudzi, Tuku, or Kutu (the thin small or old dog), or

66

senior Mukosoro (senior cougher), coughing out his plea to the skies, to his God. To be aware of the sound of the cougher in Tuku with our ears, to be told about, to listen to, listen to and hear that voice inside your heart before it dies
Everything dies inside some kind of voice
Different voices respond to knocked-on silences
Knock, knock, knock....

This poem is about voices existing in ever shifting states
Between embodiment and disembodiment
Embodiment, Disembodiment:
Embodiment is to give a physical or visible form to an idea or quality, like a voice, the voice, which is God, becoming flesh in *Jesus* (I am not talking of my friend, *Ricardo Jesus Felix Rodriguez*), embodying the word, or voice again, easily into the believers (Christians... I don't want to be unfair to *Mohammad*) hearts, include or contain as a part of a whole. Disembodiment is to separate from body, or existing without body, coming from a person who cannot be seen. God, the father, as fire, floods, Us, in resurrection. Noah! Even our Noah's boats, our airy words, our bodies, are frail against the storms of the voice. You are reading me here but you cannot see me. I am disembodied in this text, in these words, in this voice. I didn't say I am dead!
It is a state where the leaf
Flying in the wind says something
It would hear itself
A voice that lets nothing speaks to you
To itself
A voice that lets nothing touches what the story truly says
A voice that lets nothing feels what the story truly means
It is a voice as body, as un(em)body, as text (untext), as sound ((un)sound)

Does it look like I care you are shaking your head, exasperated by
my *ungramaticalessness*!

We think in words, in voices
Inside us, in languages
In civilizations, in cultures, in knowledges…
In knowledge, and in this voice, compelled by hunger
We leave the cloud of ignorance, which is a cloud of despair.
Flip flop is how our movement sounds
What if all that is here, had not been there
Where an attractive sincere insincerity
Kills the pride of these accomplished things
Does not inspire value to the process

This poem is about how voices emerges out of nothingness
To be nothing, not at all
Can we quantify nothingness?
To have no voice is to talk in the language of nothingness
To create unbeingness in Beingness
This voice, in the unbeing
Is before human
What we see in the sky is a void voice
Before word, that is God
For never can we read the heavenly voice
Before sound
Before Eden
Before the big nothing
Nothingness

To be oneself, to be something
To have a voice
It's the first being; to have a voice
It immediately assumes

A second being
A listener, it is me interpreting this voice, it is you hearing this voice
A listener is someone who gives attention to sound, make an effort to hear something, responds to advice, listening to word, to the voice.
Rocxette, the Swedish rock band, in the song, *Listen to your heart*.
This other that listens is
Self, paradoxical being
Can never truly be known
The voice is this being, in this being
Is post-human?

It arises in the slow time
In concentration, thought, craft
Gathering its evidence, luminality, limns in
Experimentation
Utility

It is the voice as notes, sketches
Broken down
By instruments of
Tensile thought, itself

We hear a voice
In the middle of intimacy, as of a boy and girl
Talking to itself
Finding its own existence
Like a paradox
It comes alive, unexplainable

This voice suffers
Like angels, the Lucifer
It wants power

Of being, wording
Talking, listening

This voice exists
As part machine
Part romantic
As any poetic adventure
It must exist

The voice doesn't exist
It dissolves, blue incense
Foam thick, it is fog, soupy fog
Driven off the mountain's slopes
By a gunning 4*4

The voice decays
Through the process
From unbodiment to embodiment, from
Embodiment to
Disembodiment, to
Unbodiment;
Is simply no body (I didn't say nobody), never like before, never
after big bang (nothingness), creation. The voice before the before
you know;
Was it silence knocking upon silence for an answering voice---
silence?
Until the first speech, the air says: spring
The air taking over spring's body
The air leaving behind winter's body

The musics of this voice is found
In standalone through lines
Through-thoughts, through-words

Allowed to intersect, to impose
Each over the other
Creating a new measure

The voice forms
Stretches of thought
Is an idea or opinion produced by thinking (I am talking of
thought), or that occurs suddenly in the mind, the process of
thinking, an intention, hope or idea of something
Language through-thoughts
To the breaking point
Of wording, listening, of being

The voice forms
Stretches of thought
Thought through-language
To the breaking point
Of non-words, non listening
Unbeing

It doesn't hear
It doesn't record
It isn't spoken
It isn't heard
It is a state of
Permanence

This voice begins to hear
Patterns of sound
It records them
In words, on sheets
Of paper, like this one
In the mind

This voice is anti-voice
Is capable, happens
Creates immense sensitivity
For the tragic irony
Of human
Miscommunication

The voice is a no-voice
It is incapable
Of sensitivity, of
Beingness
Of irony, tragically
Excommunicating (Pope's style)
Uncommunicating, is it
Miscommunicating?

It achieves radiance
It accomplishes explorations
It bounds off to the unknown
It is a known
In an unknown

The birth of human apparatus
Language, civilizations, cultures
Is an over-arching dream
Capacitating, it is observed
In leapy, bounty, large pieces
Numbers, degrees, decimals…

The decay of human apparatus
Language, civilizations, cultures
Is an interval

Its displacement, observed
In fractional, fragmentary
Pieces small, decimals small
Degrees small

This voice is grace
Grace is a half-life
The voice is a state
The grace is its stage
Decayed, incurred
Through perfection
Through imperfection
From perfection
From imperfection

The voice before pronouns
The voice after pronouns
Slippages, death
New words flitter, type, titters
Unknown words flutter, furls, flying
Words in wrong places float, fluid, water
Flowing onto each other

The voice
Creates ideas
Creates dialogues
Images into life
Images into conflict
Images into dissolution
It is resisted until it reaches a state of softened sincere insincerity
It is ironized until it doesn't hurt much
It is incepted to become words: language, civilizations, cultures…
It is killed, in a machine-death

The words break down the notion of this voice
The machine of me, like a knife cutting into the thick of things,
breaks down the notion of this voice

This voice creates the-beyond-three-persons-worlds
In half-heard words that lie like dust gathered in the shadows
It creates the fourth person
Nothing addressing itself
Xe and *Xis*
Fourth person talking of
Third person's actions.
Beingness
As if
They were the third person
Themselves; herself, himself

It creates the fifth person
Vo, vo, vos,
By avoiding the cul-de-sacs and corners of unwanted possessions
Of complex feedback
Of complex cycles
Circles occurring
It would seem
Indefinitely

It creates the sixth person
Of impossible feedback
Of impossible cycles
Circles occurring
Indefinitely
In the seventh, eighth...
ze, fir, firs, ne, mir, mirs
epicene pronouns. Persons

In a voice not full of words,
But still saying a story more powerful than words.

The voice before first person world
The voice after the third person
It's as if, the addresser
Were one of you
One of us; *What if God was one of us*, Joan Osborne in the 90s song
Is an intimate, definite you?
Defining you.
Can you tell yourself by the trails I have left across these definitions?
Addressing yourself
As a no one
As a no person
As nothing

Publisher's list

If you have enjoyed *A Portrait of Defiance*, consider these other fine books from Mwanaka Media and Publishing:

Cultural Hybridity and Fixity by Andrew Nyongesa
The Water Cycle by Andrew Nyongesa
Tintinnabulation of Literary Theory by Andrew Nyongesa
I Threw a Star in a Wine Glass by FethiSassi
South Africa and United Nations Peacekeeping Offensive Operations by Antonio Garcia
Africanization and Americanization Anthology Volume 1, Searching for Interracial, Interstitial, Intersectional and Interstates Meeting Spaces, Africa Vs North America by Tendai R Mwanaka
A Conversation..., A Contact by TendaiRinos Mwanaka
A Dark Energy by TendaiRinos Mwanaka
Africa, UK and Ireland: Writing Politics and Knowledge ProductionVol 1 by Tendai R Mwanaka
Best New African Poets 2017 Anthology by Tendai R Mwanaka and Daniel Da Purificacao
Keys in the River: New and Collected Stories by TendaiRinos Mwanaka
Logbook Written by a Drifter by TendaiRinos Mwanaka
Mad Bob Republic: Bloodlines, Bile and Crying Child by TendaiRinos Mwanaka
*How The Twins Grew Up/MakurireAkaitaMapatya*by MilutinDjurickovic and TendaiRinos Mwanaka
Writing Language, Culture and Development, Africa Vs Asia Vol 1 by Tendai R Mwanaka, WanjohiwaMakokha and Upal Deb
Zimbolicious Poetry Vol 1 by Tendai R Mwanaka and Edward Dzonze
Zimbolicious: An Anthology of Zimbabwean Literature and Arts, Vol 3 by Tendai Mwanaka
Under The Steel Yoke by JabulaniMzinyathi
A Case of Love and Hate by ChenjeraiMhondera

Epochs of Morning Light by Elena Botts
Fly in a Beehive by ThatoTshukudu
Bounding for Light by Richard Mbuthia
White Man Walking byJohn Eppel
A Cat and Mouse Affair by Bruno Shora
Sentiments by Jackson Matimba
Best New African Poets 2018 Anthology by Tendai R Mwanaka and Nsah Mala
Drawing Without Licence by Tendai R Mwanaka
Writing Grandmothers/Escribiendo sobre nuestras raíces:Africa Vs Latin America Vol 2 by Tendai R Mwanaka and Felix Rodriguez
The Scholarship Girl by Abigail George
Words That Matter by Gerry Sikazwe
The Gods Sleep Through It by Wonder Guchu
*The Ungendered*by Delia Watterson
The Big Noise and Other Noises by Christopher Kudyahakudadirwe
Tiny Human Protection Agency by Megan Landman

Soon to be released
Ghetto Symphony by MandlaMavolwane
Of Bloom Smoke by Abigail George
Sky for a Foreign Bird by FethiSassi
*Dengareshiriyokunzekwenyika*by FethiSassi
Where I Belong, moments, mist and song by SmeethaBhoumik

Nationalism: (Mis)Understanding Donald Trump's Capitalism, Racism, Global Politics, International Trade and Media Wars, Africa Vs North America Vol 2 by Tendai R Mwanaka
Ashes by Ken Weene and Umar O. Abdul
Ouafa and the Thawra: About a Lover From Tunisia by Arturo Desimone
Thoughts Hunt The Loves/PfungwadzinovhimaVadiwa by JetonKelmendi
When Escape Becomes the only Lover by Tendai R Mwanaka

https://facebook.com/MwanakaMediaAndPublishing/

Printed in the United States
By Bookmasters